KU-033-235

The Life-Planning Workbook

Living your life by choice instead of chance

Peggy Vaughan & James Vaughan, Ph.D.

Dialog Press
Santee, California

Copyright © 2012 by Peggy Vaughan and James Vaughan, Ph.D.
All rights reserved. No part of this publication may be reproduced, distributed, or transmitted in any form or by any means, including photocopying, recording, or other electronic or mechanical methods, without the prior written permission of the publisher, except for making a copy for your personal use and in the case of those holding an Associate License, and with respect to brief quotations and certain noncommercial uses permitted by copyright law. For other permission requests, write to the publisher.

Published by Dialog Press

ISBN 978-0-936390-25-3

Ordering information: Single copies may be ordered from Amazon.com
                        Bulk orders may be ordered from life-planning101.com

DIALOG PRESS
9249 Carlton Oaks Dr. #44
Santee, CA 92071
life-planning101.com

CONTENTS

INTRODUCTION

Life is a journey—not a destination.

    The Life-Planning Workbook is a tool to help you live your life by *choice* instead of chance. It can help you take stock of where you are as a function of where you've been, decide where you want to go, and make specific, realistic plans to get there. It's designed to raise your awareness of how you can create the life you want. Like most other tools, it works if you work.

    Planning the life you want and taking responsibility for making it work is an ongoing process. It's probably the final stage of your development as a mature adult. It means giving up the wishful thinking of childhood that everything will turn out all right—that someone will take care of you—and accepting the reality that life is what you make it.

There are many different ways to live:

You can drive a big car and devote a lot of time to accumulating material wealth,
>   *—or you can take a bus and travel lightly, unencumbered by a lot of things.*

You can work for a large company and devote your life to climbing the corporate ladder,
>   *—or you can be an entrepreneur and work for yourself.*

You can get married and raise a family,
>   *—or you can live alone.*

You can live in the heart of a city, surrounded by a man-made environment,
>   *—or you can live in the country, surrounded by nature.*

You can live your entire life in the community where you were born,
>   *—or you can be a gypsy and live in many different regions and countries.*

There is a hitch. You can have most *anything* you want, but you can't have *everything* you want—at least not all at once. You have to choose, and ***every choice has consequences.*** You can have the big car, but you may have to forgo the feeling of traveling lightly. You can climb the corporate ladder, but you may have to restrict the way you use your time for other things. You can get married, but in doing so, you're probably giving up some of the freedoms you would have in living alone. You get the idea. There are tradeoffs in every life decision.

Of course there are many shadings between the choices described above and these are only a few examples of the many decisions you make on an ongoing basis in forming your lifestyle. ***Many lifestyle decisions are not made consciously.*** Some of them were made for you by your parents at a time when you had little or no awareness of their significance. Most parents try to give their children a good start, but it doesn't always work out that way. It's up to you either to continue your current direction or to change it if you don't like the way it's going.

How do you feel about your current lifestyle?

- Do you sometimes have a vague feeling you're not getting all you could from life or that you're living a lifestyle that's not really of your own choosing?

- Do you need to make some major decisions about your work or your life?

- Are you generally satisfied with the way things are going, but think you could improve your life by fine-tuning in some areas?

- Are you curious about how you developed the particular values and priorities you hold?

- Do you have a secret fantasy you've thought about for a long time, but never realistically thought you could achieve?

- Would you like to be clearer about your options so you can decide for yourself the direction to take with your life?

Deciding what to do with your life is made more complex today by the rapid changes taking place all around us. Careers come into being and die out at ever-increasing speeds. Developments in communication and transportation have expanded our horizons and made us more aware than ever before of the rich diversity of human lifestyles. Television and the internet remind us daily of this diversity.

That's the good news—you have many choices. You don't have to limit your career or lifestyle to those chosen by your parents or those offered by the community you grew up in. The bad news is, with so many choices, it's difficult to decide. Choosing one path may mean forgoing another, and the choice must often be made without any clear knowledge of how either choice will ultimately affect your life.

There are several key assumptions underlying this book:

1. *The potential of every person is virtually unlimited and, for practical purposes, unmeasurable.* We are skeptical of the usefulness of aptitude tests to determine what occupational fields a person is best suited for. People demonstrate every day that a strong desire to succeed in a task that has meaning for them can overcome many apparent deficits in aptitude or potential.

2. *Every person has the capacity to realistically size up their experience, skills, likes and dislikes, values, commitments, and goals—and arrive at choices that are responsible and satisfying.* We never said it was easy. It's not. It's hard work, but it's within the reach of anyone who's ready to take charge of their lives.

3. *Decisions which have been made can be unmade.* You need not remain locked into career or lifestyle choices you made in the past. Even as little as a generation ago, it was assumed that a career commitment was for life. Changing careers in midstream was often described as dropping out and was thought by many to suggest a weakness in character. Not so anymore. It's more likely to be viewed today as a sign of courage to strike out in a new direction and realize more of your potential.

4. *It makes good sense to plan your life and use all the resources at your disposal to achieve your goals.* In the final analysis you're responsible for whatever life experience you have. You can play it safe and take whatever comes your way or you can take the risk of trying to make it happen the way you want it to. Why not go for it? You can do almost anything if you're willing to set clear, realistic priorities and focus your energy on achieving them.

5. *Finally, life and life planning can and should be fun.* Taking charge of your life is a significant life decision, but it need not lead to an overly serious approach to life. In fact you owe it to yourself to create a life experience that includes a good dose of fun and joy, and you're the only one who can do that reliably. Allowing others to set your goals and priorities is to assume that they can figure out what's important to you. It seldom works. Do yourself a favor. Chart your own course, and take full responsibility for making your life work.

HOW TO USE THIS BOOK

***The Life-Planning Workbook* is divided into four parts, each one posing a question:**

Part one: *Where have you been?*

Part two: *Where are you now?*

Part three: *Where do you want to go?*

Part four: *How do you plan to get there?*

Part one *(Where Have You Been?)* guides you through a review of your life up to the present time. The goal of this reflection is to gain perspective about the ways in which your past influences your current view of the world. The focus is not on *analyzing* what was good or bad about your past, but on *understanding* its impact on your life.

Part two *(Where Are You Now?)* is by far the largest section of the book. It contains a series of activities to help in assessing where things stand in your life right now. The reason for so many activities about your current situation is because each one provides a snapshot, but all the snapshots combined allow you to see the full picture. Answering the questions about your current lifestyle will give you a clearer sense not only of what's happening in your life at the present time, but also how you feel about the way things are going.

Part three *(Where Do You Want To Go?)* leads you through an examination of the major areas of your life as they are now compared to where you'd like them to be. It also helps you look at your life from a broad perspective, clarifying what you want your time on earth to have meant when you reach the end of your life. All this will prepare you to identify areas in which you need to make some choices and help you in setting goals for the future.

Part four *(How Do You Plan To Get There?)* focuses on taking the necessary actions to reach your goals. This is "where the rubber meets the road"—the point at which your goals either move toward becoming a reality or remain only as elusive dreams. You will systematically plan your actions, with an eye toward identifying potential problems that could hurt your efforts as well as potential supporters who could help make your dreams come true.

By working through the book in a serious, organized way, you can take control of your life right now. But more important, you will learn a *process* for the kind of ongoing planning that will make your life more satisfying and meaningful.

Using This Workbook with Your Partner

The workbook is organized so that individuals can work with it independently, but you can no doubt see that it can be a great tool for building intimate relationships and clarifying the kind of life you and your partner are trying to create together. Just how beneficial it is in this regard will depend in large measure on how you use it.

First, a word of caution. No matter how well you know each other at this point, you can expect to learn some new things about your partner and yourself—from the past, the way you see your lives right now, and the hopes you have for the future. The *life-planning* material will give you the opportunity to explore your innermost hopes and fears. It deserves the utmost in respect when you decide to share this kind of exploration with another person.

Here are some specific suggestions to enhance the use of the workbook with your partner.

1. It is crucial for each of you to work independently with your own personal copy of the workbook in order to learn all you need to know about your own values and goals. Once you've committed your thoughts to writing, sharing them with your partner will often bring even more clarity and insight. Don't underestimate the value of writing your own thoughts down first. It may seem easier to simply share your thoughts verbally, but you will each lose some important personal insights if you do that before recording your independent thoughts.

2. Find a pace of working through the material that's comfortable for both of you. This kind of work can be very enlivening, but it can also be emotionally draining. Try to respect your differences in needs, interests, and personal styles. You may feel finished with a particular activity just as your partner is digging into it. You'll both need to exercise your best skills as non-judgmental listeners to gain the most from the experience. Generally speaking, sharing smaller chunks frequently will work better than larger chunks with more time in between.

3. Use care in choosing where you work on the workbook together and the amount of time you allow for it. This is not trivial stuff. It's your life and your future. The important thing is to find a time and place where you can be present for each other and relatively free from interruptions.

4. Give life planning the place it deserves in your life. Life planning is not a one-time exercise to be done, discussed, and put away. By making it a way of life, you and your partner can use this *kind* of clarification and sharing as a tool in maintaining your connection, building your closeness, and creating the life you choose together.

What You Will Learn From the Life-Planning Process

- You have the power to create the life of your choosing. It is not necessarily simple and it will not always be easy—it will always be possible.

- You have the capacity to think clearly—to put your life in perspective—to act on sound values—to live responsibly and well.

- You are a worthy person with the right and the ability to choose your own course. You can probably have anything you want, but not everything you want.

- You are not your past, but you are a product of it. Who you are may be your parents' fault, but if you stay that way, it's your own fault. No parents are perfect; most do the best they can; in the process they do some things well and some things poorly.

- The truth is, many people have shaped you into the person you are today, but you have the opportunity and responsibility of determining the person you will become. If you ever hope to take full responsibility for your life, you must come to an easy acceptance of your past and the way it has shaped you.

- You are a potent person with a rich set of experiences. You are a survivor. You are a learner. You are unique. No one looks at the world exactly the same way you do. The way you view the world and what's possible is a function of what you've learned and experienced—and the way you put it all together.

- In a few important respects, we are all the same. We share the same basic needs. We all have the same amount of time—24 hours a day—to pursue our goals.

- The way you focus your attention makes all the difference. You energize yourself with good choosing and depress yourself with poor choosing. Awareness is crucial to good choosing, but movement is the key to effective living—knowing which awareness to act on and when to move on.

- We all change—choosing and changing are inevitable. Not to choose is a choice. Not to change is impossible. The choices you make every day—big ones and little ones—determine the quality of your life today and your possibilities for the future.

- Work is as natural to human beings as play. You need both all your life. Find the work you can be passionate about. Find the play that enables you to be a good animal—fit and supple. The roles you play are one way you think of your self-image, but they do not define your essence.

- We all suffer loss—the only question is how you will deal with it when it comes your way. You can learn and grow from it or you can feel sorry for yourself and diminish yourself. Nietzsche was right on this one: "That which does not kill me, strengthens me."

- Values do matter—they are at the heart of everything we do. Your values ultimately determine who you are and what you will become.

- We are all social creatures—we define ourselves in and through our relationships with others. Energy and inner joy come from focusing your time on people, things, and activities that you care about. You create meaning in your life by living according to your deepest values.

- Things take time. There are no short-cuts to most worthwhile goals and no quick fixes to many of our problems. Realistic planning is one of the keys to solving problems and achieving goals.

- Life is tenuous. The wise course is to pursue your highest priorities now. Happiness comes to those who pursue meaningful goals of their own choosing and assume full responsibility for the journey.

- Life presents us with many obstacles and opportunities. Sustaining focus and balance in the face of all the demands on your time and energy is an awesome challenge. Potential is not your problem; you have more than enough potential to do what you want.

- What you need is to get great clarity about what's important and organize your life to pursue those things effectively. Goals are important to purposeful living, but they need not be written in stone. Remember the proverb, no matter how far you've gone down the wrong path, turn back.

- You will get off course—and that's OK. Imitate a modern jetliner—stay focused on the destination (goal) and make many small course corrections. There's less likelihood of overcorrecting and the ride will be smoother.

- Acknowledge your ability to block yourself from reaching your goals—then don't do it. Be kind to yourself. You are not alone—others will help you pursue your dreams. You sometimes need to ask them clearly for the help you want.

- Go for it; dare to live life to the fullest. Everyone experiences some good things and some bad. The challenge for each of us is to put it all in perspective—to be nurtured by the good—to learn from the bad—to let it go—to go ahead.

- Everything is connected. Keep learning and remember rule #6 (p. 116).

NOTES TO MYSELF:

> *Most people search high and wide for the keys to success.*
> *If they only knew, the key to their dreams lies within.*
>
> *George Washington Carver*

NOTES TO MYSELF:

> *Every great dream begins with a dreamer. Always remember, you have within you the strength, the patience, and the passion to reach for the stars to change the world.*
>
> Harriet Tubman (1820-1913), American escaped slave, abolitionist, humanitarian

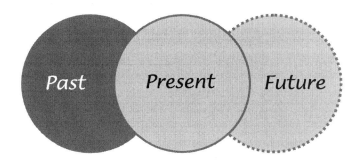

PART ONE

WHERE HAVE YOU BEEN?

If you ever hope to take charge of your life and live it to the fullest, you must come to terms with your past. You don't have to be proud of it, but you must come to an easy acceptance of it. You are not your past, but you are a product of it.

> *In the early decades, other people have more say in our lives than we do. But sooner or later, we will come face to face with the question, What am I supposed to do with the rest of my life?*
>
> *Harold Kushner*

LIFE REVIEW

The main purpose of the life review is to give you a better understanding of who you are as a consequence of where you've been. You already have some ideas about how you got to be the way you are. One or more events may stand out clearly in your memory as turning points in your life. You may also have been told some things by others, such as, "you're just like your mother." Doing a life review will allow you to organize what you know about your life experience and possibly view it from a different vantage point. We're often caught up in the events in our lives in a way that prevents us from understanding their full impact at the time of their occurrence.

Most of us have done things and had things happen to us in the past we'd just as soon forget. That's understandable, but not necessarily helpful. You are not responsible for many of the things that happened to you in your childhood, but you are responsible now for understanding that everything you experienced played some part in making you the person you are today and in shaping the way you see the world.

PUTTING YOUR LIFE IN PERSPECTIVE

☐   Before beginning the life review, take a few minutes to think about the broad scope of your life.

Is it difficult to picture yourself as an old person?

Is it even more difficult to contemplate your own death?

Your past and your current lifestyle have a lot to do with how long you're likely to live—as well as the quality of the life you're creating.

Insurance companies are very interested in how long people live. To stay in business they must be able to make reasonably accurate predictions about large groups of people.

The Life Expectancy Questionnaire on the following page reflects what they've learned about the impact of many hereditary and lifestyle issues on individual longevity in the United States. Some of the items, such as the average life expectancy (78) and the differences in life expectancy between men and women reflected in the second item, are specific to the U.S., but most of the items apply to people all over the world.

Complete it for yourself and you'll have a reasonable estimate of your life expectancy. If you know that the average life expectancy in the country/region where you live is significantly different, then begin with that number instead of 78. You may also know of personal health factors that are not covered in this brief form. Include those in your final calculation.

The goal is not to accurately pinpoint your life expectancy. Your individual situation is far too complex for that. Rather, the intent is to provide some useful perspective for thinking about where you are in your life, what you can do to improve the quality and longevity of your life and how much time you have to plan for.

In the final analysis, the lifestyle choices you make will play a major role in your health and longevity.

LIFE EXPECTANCY QUESTIONNAIRE

If you are between 20 and 65, living in the United States and reasonably healthy, this set of guidelines provides an estimate of your life expectancy.

1. **Start with 78**.. **78**

2. **Gender:** If you are male, subtract 3. If you are female, add 3. That's right, there's a 6 year spread between the sexes. *81*

3. **Lifestyle:**
   a. If you live in an urban area with a population over 2 million, subtract 2. If you live in a town under 10,000 or on a farm, add 2. .... *83*
   b. If you work behind a desk, subtract 3. If you do regular, heavy physical labor, add 3.. ...... ____
   c. If you exercise strenuously (tennis, running, swimming, etc.) five times a week for at least a half hour, add 2. .... ____
   d. If you live with a spouse or friend, add 5. If not, subtract 1 for every 10 years alone since age 25. People together eat better, take care of each other, are less depressed.................... *88*

4. **Psyche:**
   a. Sleep more than 10 hours each night? Subtract 4. Excessive sleep is a sign of depression, circulation diseases. .... ____
   b. Are you intense, aggressive, easily angered? Subtract 3. Are you easygoing, relaxed, a follower? Add 3. .... *85*
   c. Are you happy? Add 1. Unhappy? Subtract 2. .... *83*
   d. Have you had a speeding ticket in the last year? Subtract 1. Accidents are the fourth largest cause of death, first in young adults.. ____

5. **Success:**
   a. Earn over $100,000 a year? Subtract 2. Wealth breeds high living, tension. .... ____
   b. If you finished college, add 1. If you have a graduate or professional degree, add 2 more. Education seems to lead to moderation. .... ____

6. **Heredity:**
   a. If any grandparent lived to 85, add 2. If all 4 grandparents lived to 80, add 6. .... *85*
   b. If either parent died of stroke or heart attack before the age of 50, subtract 4. .... ____
   c. If any parent, brother, sister under 50 has (or had) cancer or a heart condition, or has had diabetes since childhood, subtract 3.. ____

7. **Health:**
   a. Smoke more than 2 packs a day? Subtract 8. One to 2 packs a day? Subtract 6. One-half to one? Subtract 3. .... ____
   b. Men: Drink more than 2 alcoholic drinks a day? Subtract 1. . ...
      Women: Drink more than 1 alcoholic drink a day? Subtract 1.. *84*
   c. Overweight by 50 pounds or more? Subtract 8. By 30 to 49 pounds? Subtract 4. By 10 to 29 pounds? Subtract 2... ____
   d. Men over forty, if you have annual checkups, add 2. Women, if you see a gynecologist once a year, add 2. .... ____

8. **Age Adjustment:**
   Between 30 and 40? Add 2. Between 41 and 50? Add 3. Between 51 and 65? Add 4. This is your life expectancy:... *87*

Instructions For Life Review

You will be using the Life-Planning Worksheet on Pages 18 and 19 for your life review.

☐ ***Begin by entering your date of birth and your predicted date of death*** (obtained from the life expectancy questionnaire) at the top of the circle on the Life-Planning Worksheet. Consider the perimeter of the circle to be your lifeline. Estimate where you currently are on the lifeline (your present age) and draw a line from that point to the center of the circle. This gives you a clear picture of the amount of your life you've already lived and the time you have left to plan for.

A good way to approach the next part of the life review is to pretend you're a detective. Your goal is to solve the mystery of how you got to be the way you are. Begin your investigation by writing down the "facts" of your life as you recall them.

☐ ***First, think of the people who have been influential in your life.*** Go back to your earliest memories and continue right up to the present. Don't censor yourself. Include those who had a negative influence along with those whom you remember with fondness. Write their names around the outside of your lifeline.

☐ ***Next, focus on some key events and experiences that have shaped your life.*** Recall the incidents that were significant for you—whether or not you realized it at the time. List some of these events at the appropriate time along your lifeline.

☐ ***Notice the feelings you remember in association with the people and events from your past.*** It's normal to feel a rush of emotions with such memories, but don't stop to wallow in them. You can decide to come back and enjoy the positive ones at a later time if you choose to. The important thing now is to get down all the facts—and feelings are facts. Other people in your life may not have encouraged you to express your feelings, but they were just as real as the events that produced them. Write them down inside your lifeline.

- ☐ ***What decisions stand out in your memory?*** When you were young, your parents or whoever raised you made lots of decisions for you—the kind of clothes you should wear, the kind of words you should use, the way you should treat older people, the religion you should practice, etc. At some point you started to make more decisions for yourself. What age were you then? Write down some of the key decisions you have made.

- ☐ ***Reflect on your early childhood values.*** The people who raised you taught you many of their values and beliefs about what's important in life and the way things work. You may be surprised to realize that some of the values you resisted as a child are very dear to you now. You may also be pleased to see that you've been able to change your values and beliefs as your experience and the world around you have changed. No matter how wise your parents may have been, no one has all the answers. If your childhood was painful, you may have tried hard to forget it. The idea of deliberately bringing back painful feelings and frightening emotions may have no appeal to you. All we can say is that by trying to keep a tight lock on your past, you're using energy which could be put to better use in the present. Make note of some of your early values.

Recap of Instructions:

1. Enter your date of birth and your predicted date of death (obtained from the life expectancy form) at the top of the circle on the ***Life-Planning Worksheet***. Write your current age at the appropriate place on the circle and draw a line from that point to the center of the circle.

2. Write the names of people who have been influential in your life around the outside of your circle at the approximate time they had the most impact.

3. Make note of some of the key events and decisions that shaped your life along the perimeter of your circle at the approximate times they occurred.

4. On the inside of your circle, note some of the feelings that were associated with all of the above.

5. Write down the values you learned from family members, teachers, and others.

LIFE-PLANNING WORKSHEET

31·12· 2053

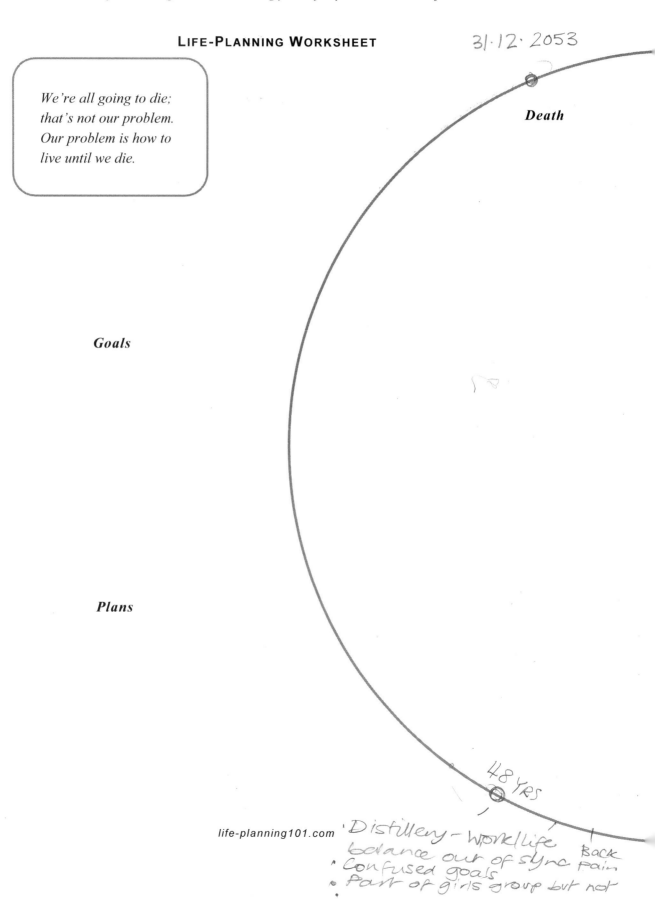

*We're all going to die;
that's not our problem.
Our problem is how to
live until we die.*

Death

Goals

Plans

48 YRS

life-planning101.com

'Distillery — work/life
balance out of sync   Back
                              Pain
° Confused goals
° Part of girls group but not

LIFE-PLANNING WORKSHEET

27.08.1966

Birth

DAD
MUM
SUSAN
GRANDMA O
GRANDAD O
GRANDMA L
GRANDAD L

10 YRS — AUNTIE DOREEN
MR HUTCHEON
CHARLIE BANNERMAN
NEIL FRASER
MR HARVEY
STEPHEN BAIN
PEIGI MCKILLOP
HAZEL O'CONNOR

Feelings

20 YRS — HOWARD DAWSON
STEVEN HOLT
ROWNTREES CATCH
TREVOR MACHELL
ALAIN
SANDRA MCLAREN
BILL
CLAIRE TAYLOR
ANGIE LECKIE
GRANDAD OLIVER
30 YRS — MUM
CALUM & NEIL
AD

MANDY MULLENDER
CALUM & NEIL
ALAIN
PAUL GREEN

40 YRS
EWAN MACKIN
THOMAS MACDONELL
ERIC PIELE
CALUM & NEIL
IAIN

Events
- Being out with Mum & Dad
- Feeling odd one out
- Being mistaken for a boy
- Uncle John's - travelling in landrover

People
- Visiting grandparents
- Playing outside
- Favourite toys - farm, shop, recorder,

Values
- Training lots
- Going to college
- Leaving school
- Not having friends.

Decisions
- Giving up athletics
- Dropping out of college
- Grandad O dying
- Mum dying
- Being engaged to Howard
- Splitting with Howard
- Marrying Al
- Having boys
- Moving to Comrie

Thinking of your life as if it were a corporation, when did you become chairperson of your Board of Directors?

- Doing stuff with Boys
- Moving to Newtonmore
- Feeling odd one out
- Unable to stick at business
- Doing garden design
- Glenfeshie - intimidation.
- AD - wanting to feel needed, instead, feeling dominated & threatened
- Al's illness - lonely

Who sits on your board now?

life-planning101.com

THE CRUCIAL ROLE OF THE FAMILY

Your family was probably the most powerful influence in your early life. From your primary family you learned:

—how to get along in the world,

—how to make friends, how to express affection,

—who to touch, how to touch, when to touch,

—how to view yourself, how to take care of yourself,

—how to be well, how to be sick,

—what to eat, how to eat, how much to eat, when to eat,

—how to talk, how to fight,

—how to win, how to love,

—who to trust, who to distrust, and much, much more—all before you had the opportunity to see that other families often do many of these things differently, that yours was not the only way.

☐   To get more clarity on your current values write down some of the things you learned about each of the areas on the opposite page.

> *What you are may be your parents' fault,*
>   *but if you stay that way, it's your own fault.*

FAMILY VALUES

Touch / expressing affection *Not openly demonstrative, no hand holding, no kissing.*

Mealtime / eating habits *Eat 3 meals a day. Home baking good, Used to binge on biscuits as teenager - some control over what I could have*

Personal hygiene / health practices *- Always wanted clothes washed more but no washing machine, so would do my own & dry it in my room*

Communication / decision-making *- Shouting. Being tested. Not offered choice - "you're doing it".*

Sex / sexuality *- Parents slept apart. No reference to sex. No nudity.*

Discipline / punishment *- Smacks. Worried about being in trouble Shouting - Cold shoulder*

Family holidays / traditions *- Unhappy visits to Grandad O, happy with other grandparents. No hols after they died. Visited U John.*

Learning *- Not good at maths, always worried about not being good enough*

Religion / spiritual development *- Hated going to church.*

Work / use of money *- Poor with money at first but learned to manage. Always wanted to spend & have more.*

Play / fun *- Played alone a lot or with Fraser boys. Tomboy, outdoor games. Didn't want to come in*

Confrontation / anger *- Angry mother, aloof father. Avoided being in trouble where poss but would do stupid things & then be punished*

Extended family relationships *No real extended family after grandparents died*

Friends outside the family *- Uncle John, Auntie Manon & Uncle Lew, Percivals. No birthday parties*

PERCEPTION IS MORE COMPLICATED THAN IT SEEMS

No two people see the world exactly alike. Each of us creates our own *reality* by assigning unique meaning to the people, things, and events in our lives. The way you view the world (your perception of things) is determined by your own personal agenda—made up of your learned, but ever-changing, needs, wants, fears, etc. In a sense, you have your own special set of *rose-colored glasses* through which everything is filtered.

On the following page is an illustration of the way two people can look at the same outer world and interpret it very differently—based on their *perception* of what they're seeing. The question of whether the glass is half full or half empty is a classic example of the way we bring our own personal interpretation to our life circumstances and life experiences.

Your interpretation of *reality* affects everything about the way you proceed through life. So it can be extremely helpful to get a clearer sense of the attitudes, values, beliefs, expectations, etc., that form your world view. Take a moment to reflect on your perception of the world based on your own personal agenda.

Things don't change. You change your way of looking, that's all.

Carlos Castaneda

REALITY—AS YOU SEE IT

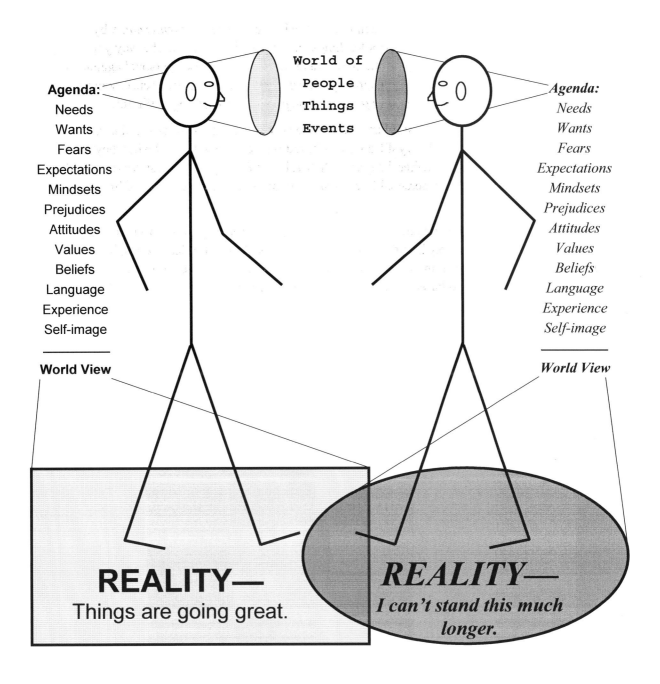

> *It was the best of times, and it was the worst of times.*
>
> Charles Dickens

HIGHS AND LOWS

Looking at your life up until now, when have you felt *most* positive, alive and excited about your life situation?

☐ Describe the general circumstances in terms of what you were doing, where you were living and who you were involved with.

When did you feel *least* positive about your life? What was your situation at that time?

> *When you come to the fork in the road, take it.*
>
> *Yogi Berra*

TURNING POINTS

You make many choices during your lifetime, some of which are far more crucial than others. A turning point is a fork in the road—a choice point that makes a difference. If you go to the right, you forego the path to the left. Sometimes you can come back at a later time and take the path you passed by, but more often, it's no longer open to you. In every such choice, there is potential gain and potential loss, and they are seldom equal.

What have been the turning points in your life to date?

Are you facing a turning point now or in the near future?

What are the gains and losses you anticipate?

> *If we all did the things we are capable of doing, we would literally astound ourselves.*
>
> Thomas Edison

LISTING ACHIEVEMENTS

☐ Make a list of your achievements.

Now is not the time to be modest. Try to be complete. The point is to get a picture of your developing competence. For example, go back and include anything that felt like an achievement at the time it happened (like graduating from high school).

I ain't what I ought to be
          —and I ain't what I'm going to be
                    —but I ain't what I was.

(Sign over a bar in a western town.)

NOTES TO MYSELF:

> *We cannot change our past. We cannot change the fact that people act in a certain way. We cannot change the inevitable. The only thing we can do is play on the one string we have, and that is our attitude.*
>
> *Charles R. Swindoll*

NOTES TO MYSELF:

> *No matter how far you have gone on a wrong road, turn back.*
>
>   *Turkish Proverb*

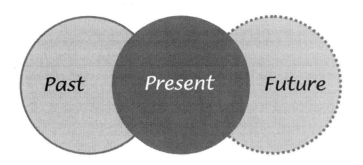

PART TWO

WHERE ARE YOU NOW?

Learn from the past…
        Hope for the future…
                Live in the present.

                        Ken Lancaster

Every transition begins with an ending.

We have to let go of the old before we can pick up the new—not just outwardly, but inwardly, where we keep our connections to the people and places that act as definitions of who we are.

Bill Bridges

WHERE DO YOU LIVE—PAST, PRESENT, OR FUTURE?

Are you attempting to live in the past because your present doesn't measure up to past accomplishments?

Are you living in fear that your past will become known to others?

Are you carrying so much stuff from the past that you barely have any energy left for the rest of the trip?

Are you waiting for the occurrence of some future event to make everything OK in your life?

Are you able to live in the present, accepting your past and making reasonable plans for the future, but focusing the bulk of your energy on enjoying the present?

WHAT'S GOING ON NOW?

It's easy to get so busy that you don't have a clear sense of just where you are in your life at a given moment. You may have a general sense of how things are going, but it's useful to get more specific about the status of some of the key elements in your life.

☐   Take time to slowly read over the questions on the following page and reflect on where you stand regarding these particular elements of your daily life.

> *There is more to life than increasing its speed.*
>
> *Albert Einstein*

WHAT'S GOING ON NOW?

1. **With time?**
   Are you in control of your time or controlled by schedules?
   Are you pressed for time or have time on your hands?
   Do you think most about the past, the present, or the future?

2. **With people?**
   Are your family relationships satisfying or strained?
   Are your friendships meaningful or superficial?
   Is your social life a pleasure or a burden?

3. **With places?**
   How do you feel about your physical environment...
   —at home?
   —at work?
   —geographically?

4. **With things?**
   How important are material things to you?
   Is your desire for things in balance with your ability to acquire them?
   Do you spend more time maintaining your things than enjoying them?

5. **With ideas and information?**
   Are you in touch with what's going on in the world?
   Are you stimulated by new ideas?
   Do you make use of books for ongoing intellectual stimulation?

6. **With your sense of yourself?**
   Do you mostly praise or criticize yourself?
   Do you feel in control of yourself or a victim of circumstances?

7. **With your responsibilities?**
   Are you in conflict over your various responsibilities?
   Does one part of your life dominate the others?
   Do you do some things just for yourself?

8. **With your activities?**
   Do organizations and institutions play an important part in your life?
   What do you do for "fun?"
   Do you choose your own activities or go along with whatever comes your way?

9. **With your body?**
   Do you take care of your body and feel good about it?
   Do you live in a basically "healthy" way?
   Do you take the time and energy needed to stay physically fit?

10. **With your spiritual life?**
    Do you allow enough quiet time to reflect on what's meaningful to you?
    Do you feel a gap between your internal life and the life you're living?
    Are you at peace with your core values and beliefs?

WHAT'S CHANGING IN YOUR LIFE?

Things are always changing; they never remain the same. Most of us have a love/hate relationship with change.

Any change taking place in your life right now that is of your own choosing, you probably like. If the change is being imposed on you, you probably don't like it—and you're probably trying to resist it.

You also probably feel more comfortable when the amount of change is a little rather than a lot. So a clear understanding of both the direction of the changes taking place in your life as well as the amount of those changes can be very helpful in your ability to adjust to them and to manage them in a satisfactory way.

☐   On the following page is a list of some areas of life where changes may be taking place right now. Think about each area and make a note as to whether the direction of any changes feels positive or negative and whether the amount of change is a little or a lot.

> *The only way to make sense out of change is to plunge into it, move with it, and join the dance.*
>
> *Alan Watts*

WHAT'S CHANGING IN YOUR LIFE?

	Direction of Change: Positive-----------------Negative	Amount of Change: A Little--------------------A Lot
Job	_____	_____
Home life	_____	_____
Family relationships	_____	_____
Health	_____	_____
Lifestyle	_____	_____
Friends	_____	_____
Finances	_____	_____
Geographic location	_____	_____
Spiritual life	_____	_____
Recreational activities	_____	_____
Fun	_____	_____
Responsibilities	_____	_____
Other:		
_____	_____	_____
_____	_____	_____
_____	_____	_____
_____	_____	_____

> *How you look at yourself determines how you look at the world.*

WHAT IS YOUR SELF-IMAGE?

Answering that question is a lot more complicated than looking in a mirror. The real issue is, how do you think of yourself? Are you assertive and confident or retiring and uncertain? Are you athletically inclined or too lacking in physical coordination to be an active participant? Are you creative? A good problem-solver? Are you socially skilled?

Ever since you were born you've been constructing your self-image. It's probably the most important construction project you'll ever undertake. The reason is simple. What you think of yourself determines what you will try and what you can do. If you think you're "no good with numbers" you may not even try to balance your checkbook and even if you try you may not give yourself a fair chance to succeed.

If you think you're not likable, you're not likely to try to initiate friendships. And when others invite you, you have difficulty accepting their invitations at face value. You suspect they feel sorry for you or they want something particular in return.

A lot of people have helped you in the construction of your self-image. The problem is, they didn't always have your interest at heart. Every interaction you've had with others and every experience you've had with your environment has provided you with raw material for your picture of yourself. Unfortunately, the foundation for this most important construction was laid during the first six years of your life—before you had the breadth of experience and judgment to make a realistic assessment of the raw materials others were giving you. You used what you were given. You had no way of knowing that the stuff you got often had a lot more to do with the self-images of your parents than with your potential. When you're 3 feet tall in a world of 6 footers, you don't question what they give you—you just take it.

Fortunately, you're not stuck with your self-image. It is modifiable. You can delete parts that are inaccurate—that don't reflect your true potential, and you can add dimensions that you haven't attended to in the past. Many of the activities in this section of the book are aimed at expanding and clarifying your perception of yourself. When you finish, you'll probably know and like yourself better than you ever have before.

WHAT ROLES DO YOU PLAY?

The roles we play are one way we define ourselves. Unfortunately, we sometimes identify so completely with our various roles that we lose touch with who we are as a person. It's important to remember that a role is only a task, not an identity. Your roles represent "what you do," not "who you are."

Nevertheless, your roles are likely to be a dominant force in your life and to exert a strong influence on your self-image. So it's important to be clear about the advantages and drawbacks to the various roles you play.

☐ On the following page is a list of typical roles. (You can add others as needed.) In the first column, estimate the percentage of time you devote to your various roles. And in the other columns place check marks as appropriate to show the impact each of your roles has on your level of energy and satisfaction.

WHAT ROLES DO YOU PLAY?

	% of time in each	saps my energy	gives me energy	gives most satisfaction	gives most frustration
Husband	_____	_____	_____	_____	_____
Wife	_____	_____	_____	_____	_____
Father	_____	_____	_____	_____	_____
Mother	_____	_____	_____	_____	_____
Son	_____	_____	_____	_____	_____
Daughter	_____	_____	_____	_____	_____
Wage-earner	_____	_____	_____	_____	_____
Entrepreneur	_____	_____	_____	_____	_____
Homemaker	_____	_____	_____	_____	_____
Lover	_____	_____	_____	_____	_____
Friend	_____	_____	_____	_____	_____
Athlete	_____	_____	_____	_____	_____
Artist	_____	_____	_____	_____	_____
Teacher	_____	_____	_____	_____	_____
_____	_____	_____	_____	_____	_____
_____	_____	_____	_____	_____	_____

Which roles are in the process of changing?

Which ones have you been neglecting?

Which ones need some planning and shaping?

QUALITY OF LIFE CHECKUP

The quality of your life experience is a function of how you're doing in several important areas—including health, relationships, mind and spirit, sense of fulfillment, and overall balance. Each area is composed of many components, so it may be that some aspects of a given area are fine while others need significant attention.

☐   On the following page are questions related to these five major areas of life. Answer the sub-questions (a through f) for each major area by circling a number from 1 (ashamed to say) to 5 (doing great) before giving yourself an overall rating on the area.

By the time you have completed these responses, you will have a clearer sense of which of the major areas of life need your attention. This will be valuable perspective later on when you reach the point of determining what goals you want to set for the future.

QUALITY OF LIFE CHECKUP

How Are You Doing:	Ashamed To Say	Need Major Tuneup	Need Modest Change	Need Fine Tuning	Doing Great
1. In Managing Your Health?	1	2	3	4	5
a. Is your weight about right?	1	2	3	4	5
b. Are you eating a healthy, balanced diet?	1	2	3	4	5
c. Do you limit your use of drugs?	1	2	3	4	5
d. Are you exercising vigorously 3 to 4 times a week?	1	2	3	4	5
e. Are you keeping your body toned by stretching daily?	1	2	3	4	5
f. Are you getting enough rest and sleep?	1	2	3	4	5
2. In Your Relationships?	1	2	3	4	5
a. Do you express love and caring easily and frequently?	1	2	3	4	5
b. Are you finding time to maintain your friendships?	1	2	3	4	5
c. Are you dealing honestly with conflicts as they arise?	1	2	3	4	5
d. Do you have a satisfying sex life?	1	2	3	4	5
e. Do you have at least one relationship where you feel totally accepted?	1	2	3	4	5
f. Do you feel sustained by your relationships?	1	2	3	4	5
3. In Feeding Your Mind And Spirit?	1	2	3	4	5
a. Are you reading enough good books?	1	2	3	4	5
b. Are you informed about and involved in larger social and world issues?	1	2	3	4	5
c. Are you exposing yourself to stimulating, new ideas?	1	2	3	4	5
d. Does your lifestyle reflect your basic values?	1	2	3	4	5
e. Do you take time periodically to reflect on the purpose of your life?	1	2	3	4	5
f. Are you finding meaning in your life as a whole?	1	2	3	4	5
4. With Your Sense of Fulfillment?	1	2	3	4	5
a. Are you engaged in satisfying work?	1	2	3	4	5
b. Are you pleased with the activities that capture most of your time?	1	2	3	4	5
c. Are you making the kind of contribution to others you want to?	1	2	3	4	5
d. Are you making good use of your talents?	1	2	3	4	5
e. Are you having fun and enjoying your fair share of belly laughs?	1	2	3	4	5
f. Are you content with what you've achieved thus far?	1	2	3	4	5
5. In Balancing Your Life?	1	2	3	4	5
a. Are you starting most days with energy and confidence?	1	2	3	4	5
b. Do you feel good about your options and prospects?	1	2	3	4	5
c. Do you have a support system that assists you in achieving your goals?	1	2	3	4	5
d. Are you living mostly in the present as opposed to the past and future?	1	2	3	4	5
e. Are you in control of your use of time?	1	2	3	4	5
f. Are you coping well with the inevitable losses that come to all of us?	1	2	3	4	5

Suppose we were to tell a man that there is a mansion ready and waiting for his occupancy just over the hill.

He wants to believe you, but he is unable to. He has been fooled too many times by too many people, and he is not willing to risk being hurt again.

But the mansion actually exists whether he moves toward it or not. Whether he claims it or not, it is always there ready for him.

This is our problem: the man will not walk toward the mansion until he sees it, and he cannot see it until he walks toward it.

Maxwell Maltz

WHAT MOTIVATES YOU?

In Other Words, Why On Earth Did You Do That?

The issue of human motivation has fascinated us for a long time, but it remains an elusive quarry. When things are going smoothly, we don't worry about it. But when our expectations aren't being met, we want to know why. Why did you tell her that? Why didn't you call me first? Why? Why? Why? The questions can be endless when someone doesn't act the way we want them to or when their actions don't fit with the way we think we'd act in the same situation.

Understanding our own actions can be equally puzzling. Who among us hasn't said, I don't know what came over me. The fact is, we're often at a loss to explain our actions to others. We don't always act as we intend to and we don't always understand why. And, of course, there are the times when we know very well why we did something, but are ashamed to admit it.

There are many reasons why it's difficult to understand the actions of others, as well as our own. First, there's the matter of complexity. We all share a set of physiological needs that we must satisfy in order to survive. The manner in which we satisfy them, however, varies a great deal from one person to another. The nature of these needs is that they are never satisfied completely. Even though you stuff yourself the next time you become hungry, you will get hungry again a short time later. Second, each of us acquires a set of learned needs and wants which continue to change throughout our lives. The list of learned needs varies across a broad spectrum even among people raised in the same family. Finally, at any moment in time, we're trying to satisfy as many needs and wants as we can. It's a constant balancing act, requiring a continual shifting of focus.

POSSIBLE MOTIVATORS

☐   The following page lists some possibilities of what may have been the motivating forces in your life up until now. Read over the list and note which ones strike you as the ones that usually guide your actions.

You might also think back over some of your successes or accomplishments as you read through the list. Which of these motivators were the forces behind your drive to succeed?

Have your preferred motivators served you well or do you feel a need to deliberately focus on others that might better support the kind of life you want?

POSSIBLE MOTIVATORS

1. To live: To eat, sleep, avoid pain, and do whatever is necessary to go on living.

2. To feel physically safe and secure: To have enough money or means to provide for a decent roof overhead and other essential basics.

3. To live the "good life:" To accumulate money and material things.

4. To have satisfying relationships: To love and be loved, to have good friendships and good working relationships.

5. To be alone: To get away from the stimulation of other people and things to rest and regroup.

6. To conform: To fit in with the crowd.

7. To look good: To gain approval and recognition.

8. To be independent: to learn enough and develop enough competence to stand on your own two feet and control your own life.

9. To experience change: To have a little novelty along the way, to learn new things and change occasionally.

10. Fear: of failing, of being rejected, of looking bad, of the unknown.

11. To leave your mark: To be creative, to express your uniqueness in whatever you do.

12. To enjoy life: To do things that are fun and/or satisfying.

13. To win: To be number 1.

14. To feel good about yourself: To accept yourself as a worthy person, to like yourself.

15. To achieve excellence: To do the best that you can.

16. To find meaning: To have a sense of purpose, to believe your life makes a difference, to find where you fit in the scheme of things.

17.

18.

19.

20.

JOB SATISFACTION

There's no escaping the central role that work plays in most of our lives. Whether or not you're currently employed, most of us spend a large part of our lives on the job. Your level of satisfaction with your job is sure to affect other areas of your life, so your job satisfaction is more critical than just its effect on your success or productivity.

It's tempting to "go along" with whatever job situation exists (especially in difficult economic times), but regardless of your current ability to change jobs, it's useful to understand just what you *prefer* in a work situation.

☐ The following page allows you to clarify what aspects of a job bring you the most overall satisfaction. As you read down the list, make notes as to which areas are most important to you. Then go back over the list, determining whether your priorities are currently being met.

When it comes time to set goals, you'll be well served by having assessed your current job satisfaction and gotten more clarity about what you want.

> *Regardless of what is changing in a person's life— marital status, health, finances or spiritual beliefs— **work is affected.***
>
> *Sometimes the change intensifies a person's energy, but more often it diverts energy from work to that area of the person's life that is changing.*
>
> *Bill Bridges*

JOB SATISFACTION

1. Mental challenge:

2. Physical challenge:

3. Contact with people:

4. Task variety:

5. Predictability:

6. Responsibility:

7. Financial benefits:

8. Security:

9. Physical environment:

10. Job status:

11. Flexibility:

12.

INTERACTION OF WORK AND HOME LIFE

You may have just determined that your job fails to bring you the kind of satisfaction you want. If that's the case, you can be sure it affects the quality of your home life. All too often, people try to divide themselves into two separate people and pretend that one part of their life has nothing to do with the other. But they're kidding themselves.

Not only does your work impact your home life, but your home life affects your work as well. The most dedicated family person can become distracted by work demands, and the most committed worker is distracted to some extent by home life considerations, especially in special times of birth, death, marriage, divorce, etc.

It's important to recognize that the impact each area has on the other is usually both positive and negative. For instance, work may have a positive impact on home life by providing financial resources to purchase a home, schooling, vacations, etc. Work may also have a negative impact on home life by interfering with time for family activities and involvement.

☐   The following page can help clarify the nature of these interactions. Fill in each of the four quadrants, reflecting first on both the positive and negative impacts of work on home life, then the positive and negative impacts of home life on work.

Notice which area has more of a negative than a positive effect on the other. What goals might you want to pursue for balancing these critical areas of life?

> *He underwent a nine-and-a-half-hour operation. On the eighth day his wife picked him up from the hospital and said, "You want to go home?" to which he replied, "No, I want to go to the office."*
>
> *Herb Goldberg*

INTERACTION OF WORK AND HOME LIFE

Impact of work on home life:

Positive	*Negative*

Impact of home life on work:

Positive	*Negative*

HOW ARE YOU BALANCING YOUR PRIORITIES?

Imagine your life is like a bicycle wheel. You're in the center and it's up to you to keep the spokes adjusted so that you get a relatively smooth ride.

☐ Write your priorities on the spokes. Add more spokes if you need them.

Which of your priorities are getting the lion's share of your time and energy? Which are getting short shrift?

Do your current priorities inform your answers to the questions inside the hub of the wheel?

Getting great clarity about your priorities is the first step in achieving some balance in your life. Staying focused and making adjustments as needed are additional steps in sustaining a reasonable degree of balance.

> *Life is change...*
>
> *Growth is optional...*
>
> *Choose wisely...*
>
> *Karen Kaiser Clark*

HOW ARE YOU BALANCING YOUR PRIORITIES?

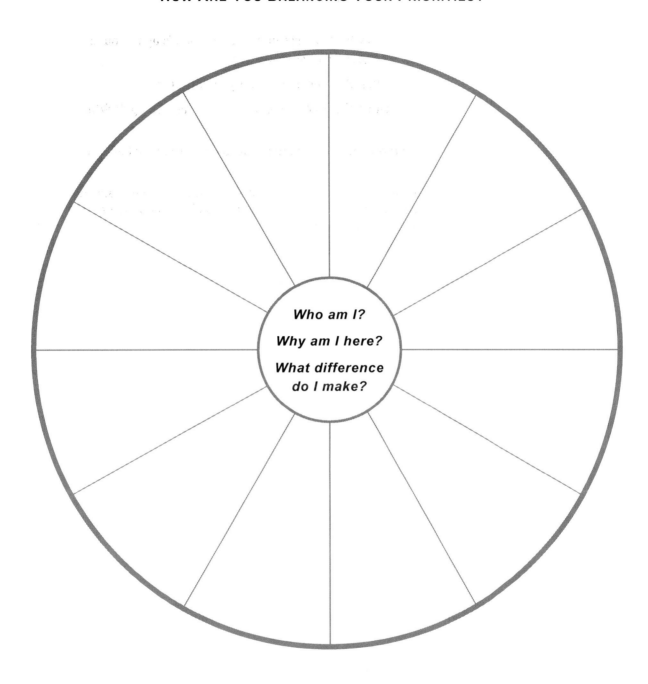

Who am I?

Why am I here?

What difference do I make?

> *Habit is habit, and not to be flung out the window by any man, but coaxed downstairs a step at a time.*
>
> Mark Twain

HOW ARE YOU USING YOUR TIME AND ENERGY?

☐ Circle a number between 1 and 10 to indicate the level of time and energy you're investing in each of the following:

Time / Energy Investment

	Low									High
Career	1	2	3	4	5	6	7	8	9	10
Spouse/Partner	1	2	3	4	5	6	7	8	9	10
Children	1	2	3	4	5	6	7	8	9	10
Extended Family	1	2	3	4	5	6	7	8	9	10
Friends	1	2	3	4	5	6	7	8	9	10
Social	1	2	3	4	5	6	7	8	9	10
Education/Self-development	1	2	3	4	5	6	7	8	9	10
Community	1	2	3	4	5	6	7	8	9	10
Religion	1	2	3	4	5	6	7	8	9	10
Guilt (the past)	1	2	3	4	5	6	7	8	9	10
Worry (the future)	1	2	3	4	5	6	7	8	9	10
Sports/exercise	1	2	3	4	5	6	7	8	9	10
Hobbies	1	2	3	4	5	6	7	8	9	10
Watching TV	1	2	3	4	5	6	7	8	9	10
Surfing the internet	1	2	3	4	5	6	7	8	9	10
_____	1	2	3	4	5	6	7	8	9	10
_____	1	2	3	4	5	6	7	8	9	10

What changes do you need to make?

• Need to spend more time:

• Need to spend less time:

WHAT'S THE BEST USE OF YOUR TIME RIGHT NOW?

On the following page is a model to help you decide how to use your time effectively and efficiently. All behavior begins with an awareness. Some awarenesses lead to positive *excitement*. In other words, they *mobilize* you to take *action*—such as getting something to eat when you're hungry. Eating the food is the crucial moment of *contact*. As soon as your hunger is satisfied, you *withdraw* your attention from eating and turn to another awareness.

Every awareness has the potential to lead to action, but not every one does. Sometimes you feel a strong impulse to act, but you stop yourself because you predict it will lead to negative consequences or because you estimate the potential gain from the action is not worth the effort. Deciding which awareness to act on is crucial. You cannot act on all of them, and you cannot know the outcome of any contemplated action until the moment of contact.

Choosing wisely is the key to effective living. Knowing your priorities and values is an absolute requirement for choosing wisely. Another important factor in the choice process is your sense of yourself—your self-image. If you think poorly of your capabilities and your potential, you are less likely to take risks in seeking the kinds of contact you would really like. A person with a very low self-image will block themselves from even speaking in situations where they don't feel worthy.

Remember, you are a worthy person with virtually unlimited potential, and you're creating your life experience by the choices you make—large and small—every day. If you're not satisfied with the way your life is going, it's up to you to get clarity and take the actions to change it.

WHAT'S THE BEST USE OF YOUR TIME RIGHT NOW?

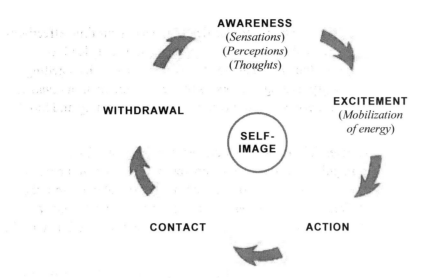

AWARENESS
(*Sensations*)
(*Perceptions*)
(*Thoughts*)

EXCITEMENT
(*Mobilization of energy*)

WITHDRAWAL

SELF-IMAGE

CONTACT

ACTION

Awareness Principles

1. We can be fully present for only one awareness at a time.

2. We are constantly organizing our perceptual environment into figure and ground.

3. All behavior is based on needs and wants, both of which are usually in conflict.

4. We are constantly choosing which need to satisfy (which awareness to act on) and therefore are responsible for our behavior.

5. There is always risk in choosing since all actions have consequences which cannot be predicted in advance with certainty.

6. We have a natural inclination to avoid pain, and we have a built-in need for closure—to finish whatever we start.

7. Fear can be a positive factor in helping us avoid some actions that are sure to bring painful consequences, but it should not stop us from taking appropriate actions simply because there may be some discomfort or the exact outcome is unknowable.

8. Processes (experiences) we don't finish may leave us feeling fragmented and may require considerable energy to keep in their unfinished state.

9. No environment is 100% nourishing—no environment will satisfy all our needs.

10. Resistance is our way of trying to change what someone wants to give us into what we want to take in.

11. The key to effective performance in specific activities and living in general is fluid movement—knowing where we are in the cycle and choosing appropriately.

SOME REFLECTIONS

It's good to stop periodically and check with that deep part of yourself that "knows" what you're doing, what you want, and what you need. You need to stop and listen to that inner voice that's ready to be honest with you if you're willing to hear.

☐ On the following page are some incomplete sentences. Complete them ***with the first thing that comes into your mind***. Don't censor your first impulse or try to re-word an idea. Just write it down as it comes to you. Even if it doesn't seem obvious at first, any unexpected response comes for a reason—and you need to pay attention to it. In this way, you can discover things that you've kept hidden or buried, and they may be clues to some of the most important stuff you need to know.

SOME REFLECTIONS

1. I spend most of my waking time

2. I feel most relaxed when

3. I waste my energy most often by

4. When I am tired or depressed, I tend to

5. The aspect I most enjoy about my job is

6. The one thing that would make me feel more successful is

7. If I didn't have to worry about money, I would

8. To get what I want out of life, I am willing to sacrifice

9. If I could change one part of my life by wishing, I'd wish

10. On the whole, I'd rather be

Everything can be taken from a man but one thing—the last of human freedoms—to choose one's attitude in any given set of circumstances—to choose one's own way.

Viktor Frankl

WHY WORRY ABOUT VALUES?

Because that's where the meaning in life is. What you value defines who you are and what you will become.

Values form the backdrop for all the decisions we make in our lives. Becoming clear about what we value gives us the possibility of directing our lives in more satisfying ways. Our basic value system was formed very early in life. Major contributors for most of us were parents and other family members, neighbors, friends, teachers, members of the clergy, and of course, TV.

While it's accurate to say our values are shaped by those who raised us and by the powerful social forces we experience, that's not the total story. Our values are not "given" to us completely. Our values continue to change throughout our lives as we're bombarded with ideas, suggestions, and demands about what's important and what to pay attention to.

Every one of us is a living value statement. The way we dress, the way we present ourselves to others, the way we treat others, the things we surround ourselves with, the work we do, the way we spend our leisure time—all these are expressions of our values. In our own unique way, whether we're conscious of it or not, we're saying to those we interact with—this is what's important.

So another reason for worrying about values has to do with the kind of influence we have on others. If influencing others in specific ways is important to us, we had best become aware of the values we're communicating in all of our interactions with them.

ARE YOU LIVING YOUR VALUES?

Your values actually exist on two different levels—your beliefs about their level of importance and the degree to which your actions reflect them.

☐   Rate each value on the following page twice: circle the number that indicates the level of importance you place on the value and mark an X at the point that represents the degree to which your actions reflect this value.

ARE YOU LIVING YOUR VALUES?

	○ = level of importance	X = degree your actions reflect this value

Low ←————————————————————→ High

	2	3	4	5	6	7	8	9	10
Achievement 1	2	3	4	5	6	7	8	9	10
Adventure / risk....................1	2	3	4	5	6	7	8	9	10
Comfort / security 1	2	3	4	5	6	7	8	9	10
Commitment 1	2	3	4	5	6	7	8	9	10
Courage 1	2	3	4	5	6	7	8	9	10
Creativity 1	2	3	4	5	6	7	8	9	10
Education 1	2	3	4	5	6	7	8	9	10
Equality 1	2	3	4	5	6	7	8	9	10
Family 1	2	3	4	5	6	7	8	9	10
Friendship 1	2	3	4	5	6	7	8	9	10
Health / fitness 1	2	3	4	5	6	7	8	9	10
Honesty 1	2	3	4	5	6	7	8	9	10
Independence 1	2	3	4	5	6	7	8	9	10
Integrity..............................1	2	3	4	5	6	7	8	9	10
Laughter 1	2	3	4	5	6	7	8	9	10
Learning 1	2	3	4	5	6	7	8	9	10
Leisure time 1	2	3	4	5	6	7	8	9	10
Love / affection 1	2	3	4	5	6	7	8	9	10
Money / possessions 1	2	3	4	5	6	7	8	9	10
Nature.................................1	2	3	4	5	6	7	8	9	10
Peace 1	2	3	4	5	6	7	8	9	10
Personal appearance................1	2	3	4	5	6	7	8	9	10
Power 1	2	3	4	5	6	7	8	9	10
Privacy 1	2	3	4	5	6	7	8	9	10
Purpose...............................1	2	3	4	5	6	7	8	9	10
Religion...............................1	2	3	4	5	6	7	8	9	10
Responsibility 1	2	3	4	5	6	7	8	9	10
Self-growth 1	2	3	4	5	6	7	8	9	10
Service 1	2	3	4	5	6	7	8	9	10
Solitude 1	2	3	4	5	6	7	8	9	10
Status / recognition 1	2	3	4	5	6	7	8	9	10
Variety 1	2	3	4	5	6	7	8	9	10
Winning 1	2	3	4	5	6	7	8	9	10
Work 1	2	3	4	5	6	7	8	9	10

Your feelings are like messengers. Until you receive their message they wait at your door.

John Gray

RELATING FEELINGS AND VALUES

☐ Think about things you have read about, heard, or seen lately that generated strong feelings.

What made you laugh?

What made you cry?

What made you angry?

What made you anxious?

What made you feel good?

What made you feel elated?

Make note of some of the values underlying your feelings.

WHAT'S THE BEST WAY TO CLARIFY YOUR VALUES?

Experience a Significant Event!

When something significant happens (whether it's positive or negative), it inevitably changes our perception of the world. And, while there's no guarantee, these significant events usually bring greater clarity about our values—about what's really important in our lives.

Sometimes this reevaluation is obvious, especially when the event is life-altering—like the death of a loved one, being fired from your job, a painful divorce, or being told you have a terminal disease. But you're also affected by the positive events in your life—like getting married, becoming a parent, getting a promotion, or achieving some important goal.

☐ On the following page, make a list of some of the significant events you've experienced and try to determine what you learned about your values in the process.

CLARIFYING YOUR VALUES

Significant events I've experienced:	What I learned from the experience:

When one door of happiness closes, another opens; but often we look so long at the closed door that we do not see the one which has been opened for us.

Helen Keller

WORST FIRST RANKING

An important way to get in touch with what's important in your life is to ask yourself what you can do without.

☐ Read over the entire list below and then place a 1 beside the item which is the worst thing you can imagine happening to you. Place a 2 by the next worst occurrence and continue to assign numbers until you have ranked all the items.

**Worst First
 Ranking**

_____   Drop down 15 I.Q. points.

_____   Lose your eyesight.

_____   Suffer a nervous breakdown.

_____   Undergo complete financial bankruptcy.

_____   Have your best friend turn against you.

What does your ranking tell you about your values?

☐ Do you tend to identify yourself through your intelligence, your independence, your emotional stability, your material success, or your relationships with others?

☐ What is the relative importance to you of events that take place through no fault of your own vs. those for which you feel a sense of personal responsibility—feeling you somehow "failed?"

He who has a why to live can bear with almost any how.

Friedrich Nietzsche

WHAT MEANS MOST TO YOU?

☐ List the 10 things that mean the most to you in your life and work:

1.

2.

3.

4.

5.

6.

7.

8.

9.

10.

*The world is full of people who will tell you what you **ought** to do. Unfortunately, they don't have to live with the consequences.*
Only you can determine what you should do by sorting through your needs, wants, and values!

WHAT DO YOU LIKE TO DO?

☐   List the 10 things you like to do most: (Don't worry about order of priority).

1.

2.

3.

4.

5.

6.

7.

8.

9.

10.

BEFORE GOING ON TO THE NEXT ACTIVITY...

There's one more important lesson to learn from the list you just finished:

☐ Turn back to the preceding page and for each item on your list, write down **when** you last did whatever it is you like to do. Make a notation as to whether it was yesterday, two weeks ago, two months ago, two years ago, etc.

If you're not getting around to doing the things you like to do best, you need to ask yourself why. And you need to determine what you're losing and what it will do to you over the long run if you continue this way.

Life satisfaction usually depends on having a reasonable balance between responsibility and enjoyment. You're likely to pay a heavy price for letting either area dominate your life at the expense of the other.

WHAT ARE YOU GOOD AT?

☐ Make a list of all the things you're good at doing, regardless of their apparent significance. (*And remember, you don't have to prove it.*)

1.
2.
3.
4.
5.
6.
7.
8.
9.
10.
11.
12.
13.
14.
15.
16.
17.
18.
19.
20.
21.
22.
23.
24.
25.

What lies behind us and what lies before us are tiny matters compared to what lies within us.

Oliver Wendell Holmes

NOTES TO MYSELF:

Reflect upon your present blessings, of which everyone has plenty; not on your past misfortunes of which all have some.

Charles Dickens

NOTES TO MYSELF:

You are not here merely to make a living. You are here in order to enable the world to live more amply, with greater vision, with a finer spirit of hope and achievement. You are here to enrich the world, and you impoverish yourself if you forget the errand.

Woodrow T. Wilson

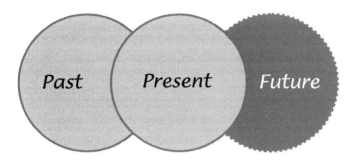

PART THREE

WHERE DO YOU WANT TO GO?

> *The future is not some place we are going, but one we are creating. The paths are not to be found, but made. And the activity of making them changes both the maker and their destination.*
>
> *John Schaar*

THE LIFESTYLE CHECKLIST

☐ Read over the checklist below to remind yourself of the multitude of issues that affect your lifestyle. While this list may not be complete, it does provide a way of getting in touch with the many areas that contribute to your satisfaction (or dissatisfaction) with life. As you read through the list, check the items that are the most important issues to you personally. Then, on the following page, choose some of those you have checked to focus on more closely. Describe "where you are" and "where you want to go" regarding some of the items you identified as most important.

Material

Food
Shelter
Clothing
Things
Money
Travel
Means of transportation
Technology
Communication media

Community

Geographical location
Place
Space
Surroundings
Nature
Culture
Responsibility
Interconnectedness

Intellectual

Ability—what type
Ability—how much
Education
Awareness
Articulateness
Creativity
Using capabilities
Theoretical/practical
Rigidity/flexibility

Professional

Talents
Training
Education
Experience

Physical

Age
Strength
Energy level
Health
Fitness
Appearance
Coordination
Body image

Social

Family
Relationships
Acceptance by others
Acceptance of others
People orientation
Intimacy
Control by others
Control of others
Independence
Interdependence
Approachability
Trust/Openness
Self-confidence
Prejudices

Spiritual

Values
Ethics
Morals
Religion
Mysticism

Emotional

Temperament
Awareness of feelings
Acceptance of feelings
Expressiveness
Emotional patterns
Motivation—needs/drives

Other Issues

Growth/risk
Fun/joy
Play/hobbies
Humor
Art
War/peace
Environmental issues
Global warming
Poverty
Authenticity/self-image
Sex
Willingness to change
Life/death
Loneliness
Time

LIFESTYLE CHECKLIST GRID

	Where you are	Where you want to go:
Material		
Community		
Intellectual		
Professional		
Physical		
Social		
Spiritual		
Emotional		
Other Issues		

ALL YOU NEED TO KNOW

The following page provides an opportunity for you to be a little philosophical about life—and to see what you can learn from your own philosophy.

☐ Read each incomplete sentence and finish it with the ***first thing that comes to your mind.*** As in a previous exercise, don't second-guess yourself or reject any of your ideas. The ideas that just pop into your mind are likely to be more accurate (on a deeper level) than a "calculated" response could hope to be.

Again, the insights gained from this activity can be used later on when you focus on making plans.

The great use of life is to spend it for something that will outlast it.

William James

ALL YOU NEED TO KNOW

1. The single most important thing in the world to me is

2. The purpose of life is

3. My greatest talent is

4. The greatest contribution I could make in this world is

5. I try very hard each day to

6. The 3 things I would like to accomplish most in my lifetime are

7. The single greatest truth I have uncovered in life is

8. My goal for the next 5 years is to

9. My greatest blessing is

10. When I am 70 years old, I would like to look back on my life and think

Live as if you were living already for the second time and as if you had acted the first time as wrongly as you are about to act now.

Viktor Frankl

IF I COULD LIVE IT OVER

By Nadine Stair (age 85)

If I had to live my life over again,
     I'd dare to make more mistakes next time.

I'd relax. I would limber up.
     I would be sillier than I have been this trip.

I would take fewer things seriously.
     I would take more chances. I would take more trips.

I would climb more mountains, swim more rivers.
     I would eat more ice cream and less beans.

I would perhaps have more actual troubles,
     but I'd have fewer imaginary ones.

You see, I'm one of those people who live seriously and sanely,
     hour after hour, day after day.

Oh, I've had my moments. And if I had it to do over again,
     I'd have more of them.
In fact, I'd try to have nothing else, just moments, one after another,
     instead of living so many years ahead of each day.

I've been one of those persons who never goes anywhere without
     a thermometer, a hot water bottle, a raincoat and a parachute.
If I had it to do again, I would travel lighter than I have.

If I had to live my life over, I would start barefoot earlier in the spring
     and stay that way later in the fall.

I would go to more dances.

I would ride more merry-go-rounds.

I would pick more daisies.

WRITING YOUR OBITUARY

☐ First, write your obituary on the following page as you think it might appear if you died right now. Remember, an obituary is a notice of the death of a person, usually with a brief biographical sketch, cause of death, and reference to close family and/or friends.

☐ Next, imagine you live until your projected age as predicted by the life expectancy form. Write the obituary you think would appear at that time.

> *O people, you are dying! Live while you can. But don't delay, time is not on your side. How could I not be among you?*
>
> *Ted Rosenthal*

WRITING YOUR OBITUARY

Obituary if I died right now:

Obituary if I live until my normal life expectancy:

What life experiences were included in the second obituary that were missing from the first?

What steps might you take to increase the chances of having these experiences?

> *There is no way to prevent dying. But the cure for the fear of death is to make sure that you have lived.*
>
> *Harold Kushner*

If Only...

Imagine you've just been told you have a terminal illness and only have a month to live. What would feel the most unfinished about your life?

☐ Describe your thoughts in terms of "If only..." ("If only I had..." or "If only I could...")

If only...

If only...

If only...

If only...

If only...

There is always sunshine, only we must do our part; we must move into it.

Clara Louise Burnham

MAKING IT HAPPEN

What stands out as your strongest wish for your life when you look at your answers to "if only?"

What goals might you set for yourself that would move you toward achieving that wish?

What might stop you from actively working toward these goals?

How important is it to you to work toward eventually finding a way to fulfill your wish for your life? (Try to be as honest with yourself as possible; don't give up unless you acknowledge that whatever is standing in your way is in fact more important to you than achieving your "if only.")

CHOICES

We always have a choice—but it doesn't always feel that way because our predictions of the consequences are so unattractive.

When the consequences are relatively inconsequential, it makes the choice rather easy. But when the consequences are life-determining, the choices become quite hard to make. Most choices fall somewhere in between easy and hard, between inconsequential and life-determining.

☐   On the following page, list some choices you want or need to make, and beside each one, place a mark at the appropriate place on the continuum to represent the degree of difficulty involved. This kind of exercise can help you focus more clearly on what's involved in making the choices that stand before you.

It's true that most choices involve tradeoffs, but don't let that stop you from acting. Remember, *not choosing* is also a choice.

> *You can have most **anything** you want,*
>
> *but you can't have **everything** you want.*

CHOICES

Choices I Need To Make: **Degree of Difficulty:**

_____   **Easy**-------------------------------**Hard**

_____   **Easy**-------------------------------**Hard**

_____   **Easy**-------------------------------**Hard**

_____   **Easy**-------------------------------**Hard**

_____   **Easy**-------------------------------**Hard**

_____   **Easy**-------------------------------**Hard**

_____   **Easy**-------------------------------**Hard**

_____   **Easy**-------------------------------**Hard**

GOAL SETTING

Now that you have generated a lot of information about yourself, it's time to use that information to make sure you're heading in a direction of your own choosing. This calls for setting goals in a clear time frame and testing for fit between short-, medium-, and long-range goals.

1. Look back over your responses throughout the book to see which areas stand out as the most *pervasive, urgent, or important* for you to focus on.

2. As you identify priorities, write them down on page 97 in one of the three time-frames.

3. Check for good fit. Do your short-range and medium-range goals lead toward your long-range goals or are they working at cross purposes? If there are discrepancies in this fit, make whatever changes are needed. If there is not enough specificity in your short- and medium-range goals, ask yourself how you will know you are moving toward your long-range goals.

4. Go back to your Life-Planning Worksheet on pages 18-19 and write your goals along the lifeline circle at the approximate point in time where they fit.

This kind of visual picture of where you want to go with your life can be a stimulus for getting you there. It can also help you do some important reality checking.

"How You Plan To Get There" will be the focus of the last section of the book. Determining your goals without planning how you're going to reach them is an exercise in frustration and disappointment. But with planning and persistence, you can have the life you want.

> *If you don't know where you're going, you'll probably end up somewhere else.*
>
> *David Campbell*

GOAL SETTING

Short-range goals: (Within the next 1-2 years: specific goals you can put in a precise time frame.)

Medium-range goals: (The next 5 years: particular experiences you want to have.)

Long-range goals: (Lifestyle issues: the life you envision for yourself over the long haul.)

One reason things aren't going according to plan is that there never was a plan.

                                        Ashleigh Brilliant

NOTES TO MYSELF:

If you take responsibility for yourself you will develop a hunger to accomplish your dreams.

Lester Louis Brown, (b. 1928),
Indian writer, author

NOTES TO MYSELF:

The future belongs to those who act with commitment, persistence and positive purpose in the present.

Ralph Marston

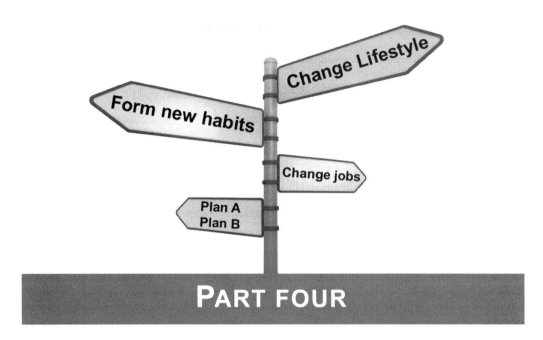

PART FOUR

HOW DO YOU PLAN TO GET THERE?

I have been impressed with the urgency of doing. Knowing is not enough; we must apply. Being willing is not enough; we must do.

Leonardo da Vinci

WHAT ARE YOUR ASSETS?

Most of us aren't very good at using *all* our assets. We tend to be aware of only a few areas of strength, whereas we actually have a large pool from which to draw.

☐ The list on the following page is intended to trigger your thinking about the many assets you can use to pursue your goals in life. By each item, make note of something about yourself in that area that you could use to support your efforts.

This is no time to be modest; give yourself the benefit of the doubt. Try to appreciate the strengths others have seen in you that you haven't previously acknowledged.

You can increase your belief in yourself by recognizing and using the wide range of assets at your disposal.

I may not be totally perfect,
but parts of me are excellent.

Ashleigh Brilliant

WHAT ARE YOUR ASSETS?

1. Skills and talents:

2. Intelligence:

3. Motivation:

4. Friends:

5. Education:

6. Family:

7. Experiences:

8. Appearance:

9. Health:

10. Material:

INDIVIDUAL EFFECTIVENESS

There are far more aspects to your ability to succeed than you're likely to have used. In addition to the personal assets you just listed on the previous page, there are many other tools you can use to reach your goals.

☐ On the following page is a list of qualities and characteristics that contribute to individual effectiveness. Think of challenges you have faced or goals you have reached that required you to really extend yourself. Make some notes as to which items on the list represent your strongest characteristics and how those qualities appear in your life.

You can see from your own experience that you don't have to be strong in all these areas; you don't even have to be strong in any specific one of them. But you do need to make good use of whichever qualities represent your greatest strength.

For instance, you may lack certain skills or experience, but more than make up for it by motivation. Or you may lack a strong personal support system, but have such strong values and beliefs that you can do it on your own. Or you may lack awareness of your opportunities, but have such strong potential that others see it and compensate for that lack.

There are many ways to achieve individual effectiveness. You can do it by clearly identifying your strongest qualities and putting them to good use in pursuing your goals.

> *Nothing in this world can take the place of persistence.*
>
> *Talent will not; nothing is more common than unsuccessful men with talent.*
>
> *Genius will not; unrewarded genius is almost a proverb.*
>
> *Education will not; the world is full of educated derelicts.*
>
> *Persistence and determination alone are omnipotent. The slogan "press on" has solved and always will solve the problems of the human race.*
>
> *Calvin Coolidge*

INDIVIDUAL EFFECTIVENESS

Potential

+

Emotions / Feelings / Attitudes

+

Values / Belief System

+

Knowledge / Skills / Experience

+

Motivation

+

Personal Support System

+

Organizational Support

+

Self-discipline / Persistence

INDIVIDUAL EFFECTIVENESS

DOING A REALITY CHECK

You no doubt already spend a substantial portion of your private thoughts in some form of planning and goal-setting. Thinking about desirable futures you want to experience seems to be a natural human tendency. It also seems to be a natural human tendency not to take full account of the gap between the present situation (where you are) and the future situation you want to create (where you want to go). If the gap is too small, the potential gain may not be enough to motivate you to act, but if the gap is too large, you may be so overwhelmed with the size of the task that you fail to act. The secret to effective goal-setting is achieving good balance between the four elements in the following model.

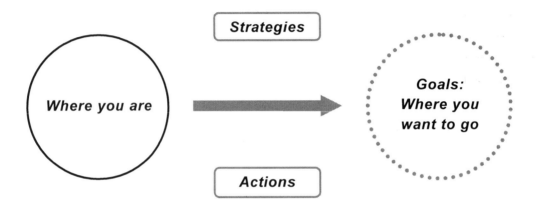

☐   Use the Planning Worksheets on the next three pages to develop specific plans for three of your goals.

Define goals that are significantly different enough from your present situation to motivate you, but not so far out that you have no realistic chance of reaching them.

Identify several strategies to reach the goal you've defined so that if the first one doesn't work, you can turn to plan B. The more complete you are in spelling out the action steps required and the help you'll need from others, the more likely you are to achieve your goals.

Finally, do two important reality checks: First, are the actions within your capabilities or can you learn them? Second, are you willing to expend the effort to learn and perform them?

> *The world is not short of people **who know how**,*
>
> *but it is in desperate need of people **who will do it**.*
>
> Maxwell Maltz

PLANNING WORKSHEET

A goal I choose to pursue:

Why it's important to me:

Strategies I will use to reach this goal:

1._____

2._____

3._____

Specific steps I will take: When:

1._____

2._____

3._____

4._____

Help I need from others: Who: When:

1._____

2._____

3._____

How I'll know I'm making progress toward this goal:

1._____

2._____

3._____

I'll know I've reached this goal when (specify an observable or measurable criteria):

I should reach it by (note a specific date):

Things that could block me from reaching this goal:

Current date:

PLANNING WORKSHEET

A goal I choose to pursue:

Why it's important to me:

Strategies I will use to reach this goal:

1._____

2._____

3._____

Specific steps I will take: When:

1._____

2._____

3._____

4._____

Help I need from others: Who: When:

1._____

2._____

3._____

How I'll know I'm making progress toward this goal:

1._____

2._____

3._____

I'll know I've reached this goal when (specify an observable or measurable criteria):

I should reach it by (note a specific date):

Things that could block me from reaching this goal:

Current date:

PLANNING WORKSHEET

A goal I choose to pursue:

Why it's important to me:

Strategies I will use to reach this goal:

1._____

2._____

3._____

Specific steps I will take: When:

1._____

2._____

3._____

4._____

Help I need from others: Who: When:

1._____

2._____

3._____

How I'll know I'm making progress toward this goal:

1._____

2._____

3._____

I'll know I've reached this goal when (specify an observable or measurable criteria):

I should reach it by (note a specific date):

Things that could block me from reaching this goal:

Current date:

HOW YOU BLOCK YOURSELF FROM REACHING YOUR GOALS

Pogo was right: "We have met the enemy—and he/she is us."

While there are sure to be outside pressures and problems to overcome in reaching your goals, we tend to overlook the ways in which we sabotage ourselves.

Each of us has our own favorite ways of blocking ourselves. In case you can't think of them on your own, just read down the list on the following page and circle the ones that ring a familiar bell. By acknowledging the ways you have caused yourself to fail in the past, you can avoid repeating the same patterns.

☐   After circling the particular methods you use to block yourself, think of ways to combat those tendencies and write them down beside the items you circled. This kind of clarity can help you anticipate self-destructive habits and avoid giving in to them.

It is not because things are difficult that we do not dare;
it is because we do not dare that they are difficult.

Seneca

HOW YOU BLOCK YOURSELF FROM REACHING YOUR GOALS

1. Conflicting desires/lack of clear priorities

2. Focus on short term satisfactions

3. Fear of unknown consequences

4. Fear of failing

5. Impatience/trying to reach ultimate goals too fast

6. Lack of awareness of choices

7. Unwillingness to accept help

8. Blaming others

9. Rationalization when the going gets tough

10. Being too general with plans

11. Procrastination

12. Lack of a consistent plan/strategy

13. Poor support system

14. Self punishment

15. Low self-image

16. Depression/feelings of hopelessness

17. Poor physical condition

18. Setting unrealistic goals

19. Being too rigid/unyielding

20. Overconfidence

21.

22.

23.

24.

25.

BUILDING A SUPPORT SYSTEM

"No man (or woman) is an island." We know this is true, but at no time is it more critical than when determining to make significant changes in your life. You need to gather around you those who will be able to support you—and be on guard against those who will (either consciously or inadvertently) sabotage your efforts.

☐   Use the following page to write down the names of some of the people who can be allies in your efforts to reach your goals. (The stronger the supporter, the closer to "ME" their names will appear in the center of the circle.) You might write down the names of potential saboteurs *outside* the circle as a reminder to avoid involving these people.

It will also be helpful to make a note by the name of each supporter as to the type of support they can offer: to challenge, inspire, encourage, etc.

Finally, be sure to talk directly to each person you have identified as part of your support system, telling them about your goals and asking for whatever specific kind of support you would like them to provide.

Oh, the comfort, the inexpressible comfort, of feeling safe with a person, having neither to weigh thoughts nor measure words, but to pour them all out just as they are, chaff and grain together, knowing that a faithful hand will take and sift them, keep what is worth keeping, and then, with the breath of kindness, blow the rest away.

George Eliot

BUILDING A SUPPORT SYSTEM

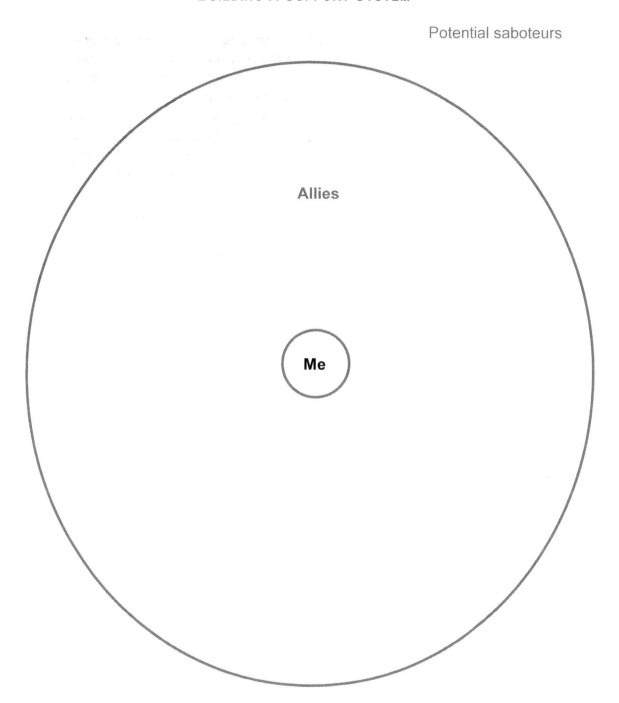

New beginnings are accessible to everyone, and everyone has trouble with them. Much as we may wish to make a new beginning, some part of us resists doing so as though we were making the first step toward disaster. Our fear is that real change destroys the old ways in which we established our security.

It is unrealistic to expect someone to make a beginning like a sprinter coming out of the starting blocks. Even when the outer situation is complete—you're on the new job, you're finally married, you're in the new house—the inner beginnings are still going on. It is a time to be gentle with yourself or with the other person, a time for the little supports and indulgences that make things happen easier.

The transition process is really a loop in the life-journey, a going out and away from the main flow for a time and then coming around and back.

Bill Bridges

AN ENDING AND A BEGINNING

This is the end of the book, but hopefully it's only the beginning for you. As we said in the introduction, life planning is an ongoing process.

If you've worked through the exercises diligently, you probably have more perspective and more clarity about who you are and where you want to go with your life than ever before. To get the most benefit out of the work you've done and the strategies you've learned, you need to continue the process.

Having great clarity about where you want to go gives you great opportunity. It does not guarantee that you will maintain the focus needed to achieve your goals. By monitoring what's going on in your life and checking this against the directions you've set for yourself, you can make slight adjustments along the way and avoid the trauma that often accompanies major course corrections that are needed when we allow our lives to get significantly off track.

A word of caution. Integrating the life planning process into your ongoing thinking will be helpful, but it won't solve all your problems. It's also important to go through an organized, in-depth assessment of your life every so often. About once a year does it for us.

While the end of the year is a good time to do this kind of deliberate reflection, it requires a very different approach from the typical New Years resolutions which are often general and vague. There's great value in going through the discipline of writing down goals and specific action plans, much the same as you did in this book. Do it for yourself.

Have fun, be gentle with yourself, and remember Rule No. 6.

Rule No. 6

Don't Take Yourself Too Seriously!

NOTES TO MYSELF:

The future belongs to those who believe in the beauty of their dreams.

Eleanor Roosevelt

NOTES TO MYSELF:

"Now" is the operative word. Everything you put in your way is just a method of putting off the hour when you could actually be doing your dream. You don't need endless time and perfect conditions. Do it now. Do it today. Do it for twenty minutes and watch your heart start beating.

Sam Ewing

ABOUT THE AUTHORS

Peggy and James Vaughan are life-long partners, both at work and at home. They grew up together in the same small Southern town, attended the same K-12 school, were childhood sweethearts and married at age 19, which they now believe was much too young. They've been married 57 years.

For the first 7 years of their marriage, James was a student, getting a B.A. in Philosophy and Religion, an M.A. in Clinical Psychology, and a Ph.D. in Social/Organizational Psychology. For the next 8 years, he taught Organizational Psychology in the Graduate Schools of Business at the University of Pittsburgh and the University of Rochester. During this same period, Peggy worked to put James through school, gave birth to their 2 children, then stayed home full-time while the children were preschoolers. When the kids were older, she returned to school to get a B.A. in Psychology at Antioch University.

In 1970 James left a tenured job as Associate Professor at the University of Rochester; they moved back to Pittsburgh and became a self-employed husband-wife consulting team. One of their first joint projects was developing and running life-planning workshops for individuals, couples and organizations.

In 1972, they stepped out of their roles as facilitators to personally participate in one of their workshops for couples. This process of identifying their values and priorities led them to make some important changes, including moving from a large Northern city to a quieter area in the Southeast with a warmer climate near the water. This was the first of many major decisions they would make using the life-planning process.

After 11 years, they again used the process in deciding to make another move—this time to San Diego, California, where they currently reside, along with their two grown children and three grandchildren

The Vaughans have run life-planning workshops for groups as diverse as the National Council of Churches and the National Defense University. They have counseled hundreds of people in the life-planning process and used it consistently in their own lives.

This workbook is the culmination of all the refinements they have made in 40 years of working with the life-planning process. It reflects their deep belief in the capacity of every person to think clearly about their values and dreams—and to choose responsibly for their individual lives and their communities.

In 2009 James co-founded a non-profit, Partners for Strong Communities, to extend the use of the life-planning process into community-building. To learn more about how you can use *The Life-Plannng Workbook* in your community, visit partners101.org.

8105831R00070

Printed in Great Britain
by Amazon.co.uk, Ltd.,
Marston Gate.